An Everyday Adventure Series
by Moji Taiwo

Grandma & her Munchkins

Seasons and their Festivals

Illustrations by Cristiana Tercero

For my precious Munchkins: Ezra, Caxton, and Amos.
Spending time with you boys brings me vitality and endless joy.

Copyright © Moji Taiwo

All rights reserved. No part of this book may be reproduced by any mechanical, photographic, or electronic process or in the form of phonographic recording; nor may it be stored in a retrieval system, transmitted, or otherwise copied for public or private use without the prior written permission of the author at mojitaiwo1@gmail.com.
ISBN (paperback): 978-1-7782838-4-0 / ISBN (Ebook): 978-1-7751235-6-9 / ISBN (IngramSpark): 978-1-7782838-0-2
Moji Taiwo
www.mojitaiwo.com

Where we live, there are four seasons and many fun festivals.
We have spring, summer, fall and winter.

What seasons do you have?

In the springtime, it rains, and the sun shines.
The grass and trees start growing, and farmers plant seeds for the vegetables we eat.

Rain and sunshine help their crops to grow.
They also plant sweet corn called Taber corn.

In spring, we went to the Lilac Parade.

Lilac is the flower of spring. So many people came out to have fun. Children dressed in colourful clothes.

We decorated our bikes with rainbow-coloured ribbons, and the grown-ups wore funny, floppy hats with fake flowers.

In the summertime, flowers b
have leaves, and the farm

During the summer, we went
The biggest was th

, the grass is green, the trees
crops grow in their fields.

any festivals with Grandma.
algary Stampede.

We saw cowboys and cowgirls on horses and wagons and marching bands in the parade.

We met happy people from around the world, dressed up with cowboy hats like ours.

After the parade, we went to the fairground.

We went on rides and ate corndogs and mini donuts.
Grandma went on rides with us, and she was not afraid.

We were so tired at the end of the day,
but Grandma was not!

What festivals have you been to?

The leaves turn different colours in the fall but fall off after a few weeks. "Maybe that is why they call this fall," said Senior Munchkin

The farmers gather vegetables and fruits to sell at markets and grocery stores.

We are so thankful to the farmers for growing our food.

That is the time Grandma buys Taber corn for us.

Sometimes she boils it in water or roasts it on a fire.

Taber corn is sweet and yummy. We love eating it!

How do you like to eat your corn?

In the wintertime, everything gets covered with pretty white snow.

That is the season for skiing, skating, and snowboarding.

"I like snowboarding and skating on ice," Junior Munchkin said.

"I want to try skiing someday," said Senior Munchkin.

"Me too," replied Baby Munchkin.

Grandma says it is good to try new things.

Grandma does not like winter much because it is very cold.

But she still took us to the Chinook Blast Winter Festival.
We saw ice blocks shaped like different animals with lights.

"I like the ice castle!" said Baby Munchkin.

"We like drinking hot chocolate and roasting marshmallows on the fire pit," said Senior and Junior Munchkins.

We have so much fun attending festivals and seeing so many people!

Can you think of a festival you would like to go to?

www.ingramcontent.com/pod-product-compliance
Lightning Source LLC
Chambersburg PA
CBHW040023130526
44590CB00036B/77